COMMUNITY · CONNECTIONS

?

WHAT DOES IT DO?
DIGGER

BY JENNIFER ZEIGER

Published in the United States of America by Cherry Lake Publishing
Ann Arbor, Michigan
www.cherrylakepublishing.com

Content Adviser: Louis Teel, Professor of Heavy Equipment, Central Arizona College
Reading Adviser: Cecilia Minden-Cupp, PhD, Literacy Consultant

Photo Credits: Cover and page 1, ©david n madden/Shutterstock, Inc.; page 5, ©Beata
Becla/Shutterstock, Inc.; page 7, ©prism68/Shutterstock, Inc.; page 9, ©oriontrail/
Shutterstock, Inc.; page 11, ©iStockphoto.com/kozmoat98; page 13, ©Racheal
Grazias/Shutterstock, Inc.; page 15, ©Iurii Konoval/Shutterstock, Inc.; page 17, ©T-Design/
Shutterstock, Inc.; page 19, ©Steve Lovegrove/Shutterstock, Inc.; page 21, ©Dmitry
Kalinovsky/Shutterstock, Inc.

LIBRARY OF CONGRESS CATALOGING-IN-PUBLICATION DATA
Zeiger, Jennifer.
  What does it do? Digger/by Jennifer Zeiger.
    p. cm.—(Community connections)
  Includes bibliographical references and index.
  ISBN-13: 978-1-60279-968-4 (lib. bdg.)
  ISBN-10: 1-60279-968-7 (lib. bdg.)
  1. Excavating machinery—Juvenile literature. I. Title. II. Title: Digger. III. Series.
  TA735.Z43 2011
  624.1'52—dc22   2010023583

Cherry Lake Publishing would like to acknowledge the
work of The Partnership for 21st Century Skills. Please
visit www.21stcenturyskills.org for more information.

Printed in the United States of America
Corporate Graphics Inc.
January 2011
CLSP08

DIGGER

CONTENTS

WHAT DOES IT DO?

HARD AT WORK

Have you ever seen an **inground** pool? How about a basement or tunnel? Pools, basements, and tunnels are all very different. But they share something in common. The same kinds of machines helped build those **structures**.

Can you guess which machines? Diggers! Digging machines help do many different jobs.

Inground swimming pools start out as big holes in the ground.

Diggers do more jobs than the ones described in this book. One way to learn more about something is by asking questions! Ask adult family members. Do they know people who work with diggers? If so, ask them about other digger jobs.

5

There are many kinds of diggers. Some dig into the ground like shovels. Others tunnel deep under the ground.

Diggers are used to build roads and buildings. Diggers push, pull, drill, and scoop. Diggers do all sorts of things!

Some diggers use big scoops to carry things.

DIGGING IN

Power shovels are one kind of digger. Drivers run the machines. They sit in areas called **cabs**.

The machine has a long arm with a bucket at the end. This bucket scoops dirt. Then the arm lifts the bucket. The upper part of the machine turns. Then the bucket is emptied at a different spot.

Power shovels can dig deep into hard soil.

Diggers come in many shapes and sizes. Can you guess why? Hint: What might a digger need to do? Move heavy things? Fit into tight spaces? Create small tunnels? Dig big holes? Would the same machine be right for every job?

9

Power shovels dig into the ground. They help build **foundations**. A foundation is the strong base of a building.

Bigger shovels are used for mining jobs. They help clear away rocks and soil to reach things such as coal. Wide, deep holes are created.

Digger buckets come in many shapes and sizes.

A **backhoe loader** can do the job of two diggers. There is a special scoop at the front. A shovel with a long arm sits at the back.

The shovel digs smaller holes and **trenches**. Workers lay pipes and cables in trenches. The scoop pushes dirt back into the trenches when they are done.

Backhoes can help with many different kinds of jobs.

Drills dig in a straight line. Some **bore** straight down to make water wells. Others are used to bore tunnels underground. Special tunnels may be drilled under certain roads. Tunnels may also be drilled under rivers and other spots. These often hold pipes carrying **natural gas** or oil.

This big drill can dig deep into the ground.

15

TEARING DOWN, CLEANING UP

Diggers don't just dig. Sometimes they tear down buildings. Their long arms can reach high places.

Diggers also move rocks and dirt. This clears the way for workers to do their jobs. Sometimes, leaves or trash collect in **ditches** and other places. Diggers can clear this away.

Diggers can help get rid of old buildings.

Diggers can also help us learn about Earth. Special drills bore deep into the ground. They bring back rocks and soil from down below.

Why is this useful? It helps miners know where to dig. Other people study the rocks and soil removed by the drill. This can help them learn about Earth's past.

Special diggers can bring up pieces of rock from deep underground.

Do you ever see people working on roads or buildings? Take a good look the next time you do. What sorts of machines are workers using? Do you spot any diggers? How are they helping to get the job done?

19

Diggers make many jobs easier. They dig big holes. It would take too long to dig them by hand.

Can you imagine digging up big rocks without these helpful machines? They save us a lot of work. What would we do without diggers?

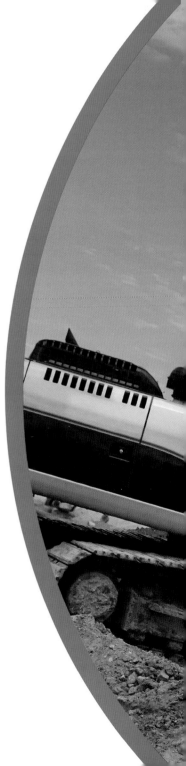

Diggers are very useful tools!

GLOSSARY

backhoe loader (BAK-hoh LOH-dur) a digger with a special scoop and bucket

bore (BOR) to make a hole by using a drill

cabs (KABZ) areas where drivers sit in big trucks or machines

ditches (DICH-iz) long openings in the ground used to supply water or lead it away

foundations (foun-DAY-shuhnz) bases on which things are built

inground (IN-ground) having to do with something that is built into the ground

natural gas (NACH-ur-uhl GASS) a kind of gas found underground and often used for heating and cooking

structures (STRUHK-churz) things that have been built

trenches (TRENCH-iz) long, narrow holes or ditches made in the ground

FIND OUT MORE

BOOKS

Addison, D. R. *Diggers at Work.* New York: PowerKids Press, 2009.

Alinas, Marv. *Diggers.* Mankato, MN: Child's World, 2008.

WEB SITES

Kikki's Workshop
www.kenkenkikki.jp/e_index2.html
Look at pictures and read more about diggers and other big machines.

U.S. Energy Information Administration—EIA Energy Kids: Natural Gas
www.eia.doe.gov/kids/energy.cfm?page=natural_gas_home-basics#natural_gas_delivery-basics
Visit this site to learn more about natural gas.

INDEX

ABOUT THE AUTHOR

Jennifer Zeiger graduated from DePaul University. She now lives in the Chicago area. Thanks for the help, Dad!

24